I0616166

EVERY SCHOOL DAY IS A NEW DAY

Short Stories of A Teacher's Experiences
BOOK 1

Leatrice D. Williams

Copyright © 2025 by Leatrice D. Williams.

All rights reserved. No part of this publication may be reproduced, distributed, or transmitted in any form or by any means, including photocopying, recording, or other electronic or mechanical methods, without the prior written permission of the author, except in the case of brief quotations embodied in critical reviews and certain other noncommercial uses permitted by copyright law.

This book is protected by copyright. You cannot amend, distribute, sell, use, quote, or paraphrase any part of the content within this book without the author's consent.

Cover Design: Leatrice Williams

Printed in the United States of America

ISBN 979-8-89114-212-1 (sc)
ISBN 979-8-89114-214-5 (e)

Library of Congress Preassigned Control Number: 2025914541

2025.09.08

MainSpring Books
5901 W. Century Blvd
Suite 750
Los Angeles, CA, US, 90045

www.mainspringbooks.com

DEDICATIONS

EVERY SCHOOL DAY IS A NEW DAY, SHORT STORIES OF A TEACHER'S EXPERIENCES BOOK 1

EVERY SCHOOL DAY IS A NEW DAY TRANSFERRING TO THE JUNIOR HIGH, SHORT STORIES OF A TEACHER'S EXPERIENCES BOOK 2

I dedicate these two books to Frank Walker, Chris Comella, and Joe Kent.

To Frank, I thank you for being strict with your staff in pursuit of nothing less than excellence and professionalism. Your high expectations never wavered throughout your tenure. The quality of your leadership was exceptional. Whatever you asked of your staff, you consistently modeled yourself. Your communication and expectations with students and parents were sincere. With the guidance and knowledge you provided, you set the bar high for your staff and pushed us to reach our full potential. Thank you with gratitude for the opportunity to teach at Elmwood School; without you as my first principal, I would not be the teacher I am today.

To Chris, I thank you for supporting me and the staff with kindness and care during your leadership days. Your professionalism was essential in reminding us of what that looked like again. As staff, we were somewhat broken due to the principals before you. I admire your belief in us and how you helped us get back on track as good educators. Your support and professionalism are truly appreciated.

To Joe, I thank you for upholding high standards of professionalism and expectations among your staff. As principal of ZCMS, always expect excellence from your teachers and students. The guidelines you established for staff and students were essential, and you consistently maintain those expectations. I appreciate your trust in me and for giving me the freedom and encouragement to enrich and challenge my students through innovative programs and lessons. I am grateful for your confidence in allowing me to offer students real-world opportunities both inside and outside the classroom to help them see beyond their community boundaries.

With sincere praise and heartfelt appreciation, these three men demonstrated genuine, authentic leadership.

Thank you, gentlemen!

CONTENTS

Note: These experiences are not listed in any specific order; they all occurred at my first school location, where I spent 27 years. However, my role as union president extended into the junior high school years.

CHAPTER 1

Inspiration to Becoming a Teacher

My inspiration began in kindergarten. I had a teacher, Mrs. Brown, who was experienced and had taught for many years. She was heavy-set and didn't move around much, but she provided us with numerous hands-on experiences, which I enjoyed. She brought lessons to life and connected them to our learning. She also had fun and laughed often. Many of her lessons were engaging and held my attention. These experiences sparked my interest in becoming a teacher.

I would go home and play school. In my basement, I had an area set up like a classroom, complete with a chalkboard, chairs, and a table. When my cousins came over, I would play school with them. We would read and solve math problems. They weren't very enthusiastic about it at all.

I was always excited about school to see what Mrs. Brown had in store for us each day. One day, Mrs. Brown mentioned that we were going to make butter. She had dressed like a woman from the past. We were surprised to see her this way. But when she sat down in front of the churn, it made sense. She added the ingredients to the churn, and my classmates and I took turns working the paddle to turn the mixture into butter. When the butter was ready, Mrs. Brown spread it on a slice of homemade bread and placed it on a paper plate. It was delicious.

(This picture is not of Mrs. Brown)

This experience put the seal on the deal of my interest in being a teacher.

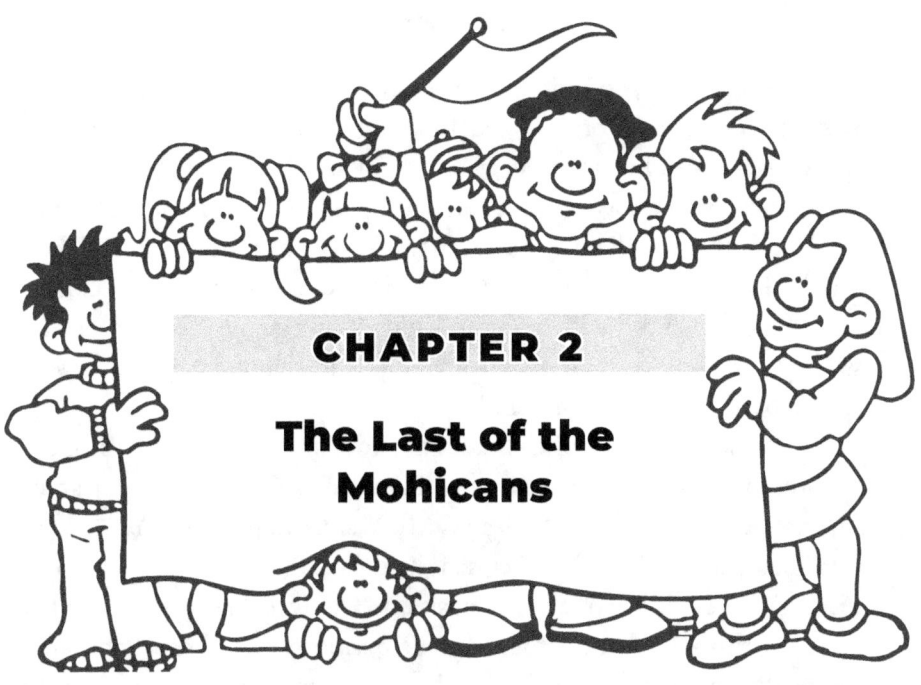

CHAPTER 2

The Last of the Mohicans

I left home in a gray suit for a teaching interview. As I drove 33 miles, I could feel the nervousness, excitement, and anticipation of the interview. Upon approaching the school's vicinity, I noticed no kids outside playing and no one walking on the streets. It was eerie, as I reverted to thinking of the sci-fi movies of all people beamed up or quarantined for some reason. I started questioning myself: Am I in the right place for a career?

I arrived at the school and parked across the street in the school's parking lot. One car was parked in the lot. I prayed before getting out. I walked to the door, and a lady opened the door for me. With a warm smile, she welcomed me in. She introduced herself as the school secretary and offered me a seat. She told me the principal would be here shortly. Ten minutes later, the principal opened the side front door and entered. He walked into the building in blue jean overalls and acknowledged the secretary and me. Mr. Walker said, "Excuse me, I'll be right back," and disappeared into the washroom.

Mr. Walker emerged from the washroom in a black suit, tie, and dress shoes. He was in true professional form to conduct the interview. He stepped to me with his hand out to shake my hand. As we shook hands, he introduced himself as Mr. Walker, principal of Elmwood School, and said, "You're Mrs. Williams." I said, "Yes." We walked into his office, he offered me a chair, and I sat. He sat behind his desk and began to tell me about the school and the direction in which it was going. He asked me a few questions and asked for my résumé. I gave it to him, he glanced over it, and looked up at me with a smile.

Mr. Walker did most of the talking, and I listened, which was fine. Then the door opened, and the superintendent stuck his head in and said, " Is she the last of the Mohican?" Mr. Walker responded, "Yes." The superintendent said, "OK," and closed the door.

Mr. Walker shared that two positions are available: a third-grade position at this school and a fourth-grade position at another school. He gave me the option of which position I would want. Since he interviewed me, I figured I would stay at this school. I gave him my answer about choosing his school for employment. He was very pleased with the answer.

Mr. Walker gave me a tour of the school. The school had two and a half floors. He shared that this school just built new walls. The school was in an open school concept environment for five years and decided to put the walls back. He showed me two rooms in which the third-grade classrooms would be. One room was oddly shaped and needed painting. The other room was rectangularly shaped and painted nicely. He asked me which classroom I would like. I chose the oddly shaped classroom. Being new, I didn't want to start with my new colleague on the wrong foot because I took the better classroom.

We returned to the school office. Mr. Walker told the secretary to give me the third-grade teacher's editions to take home. He also said to go to the district office to complete employment paperwork. I was told the school board had to give the final approval to be accepted, and the school board meeting would be on the third Monday of the month. I will get an acceptance letter in the mail. He told me the new teachers' meeting date and location. and to be in attendance, it was before the board meeting.

We shook hands. I thanked Mr. Walker for the opportunity to interview and for offering me the third-grade teaching position. Mr. Walker thanked me for coming to the interview and said he looks forward to working with me and having me as part of his teaching staff.

I left the school and went to the district office to complete the employment paperwork.

I was hired!

CHAPTER 3

First Three Days of School

My teaching career started as a third-grade teacher. My third-grade coworker was a little southern lady who was jazzily dressed and very friendly. We hit it off, and she was invaluable.

Day One - The morning consisted of teacher meetings and then lunch on your own.

Returning from lunch, I reviewed my class roster with Mrs. Franks. I said the names aloud. As I rattled off the names, I said Patrick. Mrs. Franks said, "Oh my!" I stopped reading the names for a minute and then continued. I said aloud several student names and then said, Karl. She responded with another, "Oh my!" I finished saying the last four names and placed the paper on the table. I looked up at Mrs. Franks and asked her what was with the oh my. "Well, you see, these boys are a handful of bad. They have caused havoc since kindergarten and throughout the school," explained Mrs. Franks. "Usually, the boys are in two different classes. But I see you have the two together, Good Luck!" Mrs. Franks added. She suggested that I read their school files for more information on them. I declined and stated I wanted to know the students on my own. I didn't want to taint my mind. I wanted an organic opportunity to learn about these boys. I didn't want to be biased by reading student records.

I arranged my classroom, completed bulletin boards, put student name tags on the desks, and added a welcome sign on the door. After an exhausting day, I went home.

Day 2—The morning consisted of continuous teacher meetings. I had lunch in my room, finished the housekeeping in my room, placed student subject books on each desk, and put together welcome gifts for the students. I bought decorated pencils, erasers, and rulers. I placed these items in decorative baggies with a cute note saying, "Welcome to my class. We are going to have a great school year, Mrs. Williams." Tired, I headed for home.

Day 3 -The first day of students. WOW! I'm excited and eager to get this day started. The students were on the playground playing and greeting each other. Many of the students hadn't seen each other during summer break. This was catch-up time for them.

The bell rang, and the students lined up according to the classroom number written on the ground. The teachers stood near their room numbers on the ground. Chatter between the teachers and students was heard. Once all the students were lined up, the teachers took their classes into the building.

I brought my students into the building and up the stairs. They came into the room and looked for their name tag on the desks. Once they saw their name, they sat at their desks and started putting their school supplies inside. I consciously placed Patrick and Karl's desks on opposite sides of the room. Unfortunately, they paid no attention to being apart. They started talking to each other across the room in an outside voice. I thought, oh no this is not acceptable, this won't do.

I called Karl and Patrick to my desk. They approached my desk, giddy and silly. I'm sure they thought they were in trouble in their first 20 minutes of school. I asked them to come to the other side of my desk where I was sitting. They came around the desk, silently, and looked at me. I lowered my voice and said, "I heard you two were hard workers and very helpful to the teachers. I'm looking forward to your assistance in helping me and your classmates to have a successful year. Do you think you can help me this year? The boys looked at each other at what they heard. The boys weren't sure how to answer, since my comment threw them off on what they heard. They answered with hesitancy, "Okay." I thanked the boys, and they could return to their seats. They sat down and were cooperative the rest of the day without interruptions.

Day 1 with the students was SUCCESSFUL!

CHAPTER 4

"Patrick"

You may remember Patrick. He was the one in the duo with Karl. Being part of my first year of teaching, and he's a young man I will never forget. Although he was a handful, he meant well most of the time. However, as time went on, I watched him closely and noticed that he had some learning difficulties. I believe his behavior was more about masking his inability to perform specific educational tasks by being mischievous.

Around February, I approached the special education teacher to discuss a student experiencing learning disabilities, although I wasn't entirely sure what those disabilities were. I didn't mention Patrick's name because everyone at the school had given up on him. She took the time to explain the procedures for testing a child. I took the paperwork and thanked her.

I called Patrick's mom to schedule a meeting with her. She came to the school two days later, and we sat down to talk. I voiced my concerns. She understood and mentioned that she and her husband also had concerns, expressing surprise that previous teachers hadn't reached out with similar worries. The teacher only contacted us when Patrick was in trouble.

She gave me the okay to complete the testing paperwork and stated she would sign it upon completion. Once completed, I contacted her. She came to the school and signed the paperwork. I passed the paperwork to the special education coordinator, and she set a time for Patrick's testing.

The testing time has come and gone. Now we wait for the results.

As time progressed in science, we focused on a botany unit. We planted lima seeds in soil, watered them, and set them on the counter to chart their growth.

A couple of weeks passed, and the results finally arrived. I called the parents in for a meeting to discuss the findings and plan how to assist Patrick. A day later, after school, we all gathered. The director of Special Ed, the principal, the special education teacher, Patrick's mom and dad, and I attended the meeting in a small office. The director presented the results to us. Patrick had Dyslexia, Dysgraphia, and Dyscalculia. All these "D" "ia" indicated processing disorders related to reading, math, thinking, and writing simultaneously, as well as numbers, concepts, and reasoning. The director suggested that next year, Patrick should move to a special ed class to help him work through the "Ds." She didn't want to transition him now because we had three more weeks of school before the summer. Mom and Dad were relieved to know what was wrong; now we all had an answer. They thanked me for being concerned enough to take action in identifying the problem. We shook hands. I told them I liked Patrick and felt there was more to his story, but I didn't know what it was. He had worked to the best of his abilities. Still young, I thought any intervention could help him overcome these obstacles.

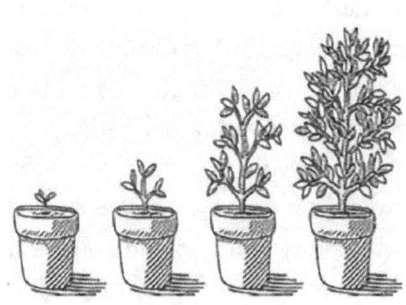

The lima beans grew. The class graphed them. Students were surprised to see how fast they grew. A week before school was out, the students took home their lima bean plants. Patrick was very excited about the growth of his plants.

The next day, Patrick came back to school beaming and told me he planted his lima bean plant in his backyard.

The last day of school arrived. Some of the students brought me gifts. Patrick was the last student to leave the room. He showed me a worn, medium-sized red satin heart with a white ribbon that read, "love you." He handed it to me and said, "This is for you." I took it and told him I appreciated the thought. Patrick gave me a hug and said, "Thank you for everything. I'm going to miss you." I got teary-eyed and told Patrick, "I'm going to miss you too. Be good and have a safe summer."

I looked at the heart and thought it was sweet that he cared enough to bring me a gift for the end of the school year. It was worn and a little dirty, but to me, it looked brand new knowing it came from Patrick.

I saw Patrick's mom at the grocery store, and she told me that his lima bean plant flourished and bore beans. She mentioned that Patrick continued to care for his science project, the lima bean plant.

To this day, I still keep Patrick's red heart in a baggie in my home office.

CHAPTER 5

The Museum Incident

My first field trip was to the Milwaukee Museum with the third-grade classes. I looked forward to this experience with my first-year class, but I fear losing a student. All the student permission slips were returned.

As the parent chaperones came into the classroom, I thanked them for joining us and gave them the students names in their group. I introduced the parents to the students. The parents called out the names of students in their group. The students assembled as a group with their chaperones.

Before boarding the school bus, I again reminded the students of my expectations for their behavior on the bus and in the museum. We boarded the bus, the students said good morning to the bus driver. They found their seats and chatted among themselves. I greeted the driver, and he replied. I sat across from Mrs. Franks. We conversed as we went down the road. I periodically looked back at the students to assure myself they were behaving and safe. The third time checking, I noticed Patrick and Karl hitting another student in the head with their caps. I quickly told them to stop and sit down. They remained seated for the rest of the ride.

We arrived at the museum. Once again, I reminded the students of the behavioral expectations and to always stay with their partners. We dismounted the bus; the students found their groups and chaperones. We walked into the museum with excited and wide-eyed students. The groups scattered in different directions. Time went by and we gathered in the museum's lunchroom. The students sat with their groups and ate their lunch. Once finished, the groups left and continued their journey throughout the museum.

About 20 minutes later, a security guard approached me with Karl and Patrick. He asked if they were my students and I reluctantly said, "Yes." Looking at the boys and the guard, I felt like shrinking Violet. I was so embarrassed and mad. This display took place on the museum's second floor with other people around. The guard told me the boys were running around yelling and saying inappropriate things. "I'm sorry to tell you this, but they must leave the museum, NOW!

I asked the guard to watch the boys for a minute to give my group to Mrs. Franks. I arrived back and relieved the guard of Patrick and Karl. I grabbed the boys' arms and escorted them to the bus. When we got on the bus, I reprimanded them up one side and down the other. They listened and then tried to explain

what and why they did what they did. Nothing they could say to erase the embarrassment I had. I told them to close their mouths and sit in different seats on the bus. Karl sat in the middle of the bus. Patrick was in the second seat from the front of the bus.

Thirty minutes or so the groups with their chaperones approached and entered the bus. The students were surprised to see Karl, Patrick, and I already on the bus. The whispering and gossiping from the students wondering why it was just the four of us on the bus when they returned. The bus left the museum. It seemed like we returned to school in record time. And yet it wasn't fast enough for me.

We drove up to the school, said goodbye, and thanked the bus driver. We got off one by one, entered the school, and walked up the stairs to the classroom. As a class, we summarized our museum experience. The bell rang and I dismissed the class. I stopped Karl and Patrick at the door. I explained again the disappointment of their behavior. I told them I would call your parents about their actions today. They left my room with no smiles or antics. I closed my door sat at my desk and started making parental phone calls.

This was an experience I do not EVER want to go through on a field trip AGAIN.

CHAPTER 6

KMART

After school, I went to KMART to pick up a few items for school tomorrow. I picked up the items and headed toward the checkout line. As I was walking to the checkout line, one of my students and her parent were walking toward me.

She tugs on her dad's jacket and points in my direction. As we get closer, I greet both of them. They both looked shocked to see me.

The student's eyes are wide, and his mouth is slightly ajar. Dad has a stunned expression as well.

They both said hello. I lean toward them and say, "You know, teachers don't live in the schools. We do have homes to go to after school."

Dad shakes off his daze and responds, "Ha Ha, that's funny! Of course, teachers don't live in the schools.

I laughed, wished them a wonderful evening, and then turned into a checkout lane.

Although we interacted, they still wore a look of surprise when they saw me beyond the classroom doors.

FUNNY! HA! HA! HA!

CHAPTER 7

The Teepee

I frequently rearranged my home in different configurations often. My classroom was similar. I get bored easily when looking at the same furniture arrangement after a couple of months, so I would change it often. I never liked rows, but I would set it up that way for testing.

Every day, the class had a planned 20 minutes of silent reading. Students can go anywhere in the classroom and read to themselves. I had a small couch in the back of the room for students to sit on but I thought we needed something else.

We read a story in our reading book about Native Americans, and we had many discussions about it. Since the students were so interested in the story, I thought we would create a teepee for our other reading space.

After school, I went to Menards and JoAnn Fabrics to purchase materials for the teepee.

When I arrived at the school, I saw some of my students outside and beckoned them to come to my car to help me get the materials out. We took everything upstairs and placed it against the wall.

The students entered the classroom, eager to explore the materials. I explained that during social studies, we would prepare and construct a teepee to create an additional reading space for their use.

Each child received a 6 x 6 inch square of iron transfer paper. The instructions required students to draw a symbol that would be ironed onto the fabric for the teepee. While the students worked on their symbol designs, the custodian and I built the teepee frame. I collected the students' symbols.

At home, I ironed the symbols onto the canvas materials. The students displayed remarkable creativity in their symbol designs. Their designs were colorful and neatly executed. I was both surprised and pleased with the level of detail and neatness they achieved.

The next school day, I left early to put the canvas material over the teepee structure to surprise the students when they walked into the classroom. Once again, the custodian helped me wrap the teepee. He was impressed once the canvas was in place. I must say it was dazzling.

The students entered the classroom with wide eyes and smiles, jumping with excitement. They gathered around the teepee, searching for their symbols. I placed two large throw pillows inside for the students to sit on. This reading area was so popular that there was a signup sheet for daily use.

It was a success!

CHAPTER 8

The Life of a Third Grader

My third-grade class has read several plays during our third-quarter readings. One student suggested the idea of writing our class play. The discussion began, and the students were intrigued by the proposal.

The discussion started with students suggesting topics and ideas for the play. After several suggestions on the chalkboard, Paul raises his hand and says, "Let's write a play." Everyone agreed.

Now it was time to think about what to write. Again, many ideas were shared and written on the board. Paul suggests the class write a play about what we do in class. Paul states, "We can call it the Life of a Third Grader." I added that we could videotape it and invite parents to the school for a family movie night. The students felt ecstatic and giddy.

During our language arts period, we learned how to write a play. After a couple of days, the students were divided into groups to write a scene for the play. The scenes include the subject areas, recess, gym, library, art, and lunch. As the groups discussed and wrote their scenes, I would visit each group for an update. I would listen, answer questions, and give guidance, if and when needed.

The class spent three days working on the script in their groups. We came together as a class so that each group could present their scenes. As a class, we organized the scenes in the order in which we wanted them in the script. I collected the groups' scenes to take home and type.

Once I got home, I typed the scenes for The Life of a Third Grader. It took me quite a while. Exhausted, I went to bed with a little more to complete. I got up early to finish the last scene and then headed to work. I made class copies for the students.

The class entered eagerly, asking if I had typed the script. Once everyone was settled and all the housekeeping tasks were completed, I distributed the script. I allowed the students 10 minutes to read through it. The room fell silent as the students concentrated on the words.

After the students silently read the script, I suggested we brainstorm how we wanted to structure our family movie night. Ideas were shared and written on the chalkboard. We decided on the date, time, and refreshments. Then we turned our attention to the characters in the script. The principal and teachers had a few speaking parts that students were voted to perform. We practiced the script for a week during our silent reading time.

Invitations were written and sent home with students to invite families to the movie debut. Parents needed to RSVP so I could purchase refreshments accordingly. For the students portraying adults, we discussed how they should dress for their roles. We talked about having a dress rehearsal to go through the entire script.

Two days later, we were ready for filming. We filmed the play in the respective areas. It took the school day to complete the filming. Done! I had a friend help me to produce the videotape. My friend and I put the title and credits into the video. We previewed the tape. It looked very professional. I asked my friend to make copies for me to distribute at the end of the presentation. I know my students are going to be pleasantly surprised and proud.

Over the weekend, I purchased refreshments for our movie night, which was set for Tuesday. The movie began at 7:00 pm. The custodian arranged the gym with chairs, placing the television front and center. The video was prepared and ready for play. I had the refreshments on the counter for everyone to pick up and enjoy during the film.

The students and their families arrived around 6:45 pm to secure good seats. They lined up to get their refreshments and took a seat. Everyone waited patiently for 7 o'clock.

I came forward at 7 o'clock to welcome the families to our movie debut and introduced myself. I provided them with background information about how and why this movie was made. Without further ado, I started the film. The families watched intently. At the end of the movie, the parents and siblings clapped and cheered. I went to the front of the audience to introduce the students, who took a bow with pride and smiled from ear to ear. The audience gave the students a standing ovation.

As I thanked the families for coming out, I informed the parents that they would be taking home a copy of The Life of a Third Grader. The students were thrilled by the surprise.

This experience was talked about for the rest of the year.

CHAPTER 9

Chicken and Hot Sauce

Snack time!

My grade level classes had the last lunch period out of three. We shuffle down for lunch at 12:45 pm. During the first three weeks, I noticed that the students couldn't stay focused and heard grumbling stomachs. I had to do something fast to keep the students engaged. The first couple of weeks I brought snacks for anyone that needed to eat to get them through until lunchtime. By the end of the second week, all the students were asking for a snack to keep going. This was getting expensive.

On the Friday of the third week, I told the students they could bring snacks. I directed the snacks to be healthy. No candy or anything with lots of sugar.

The following Monday the students brought their snacks. At 11:45 am, I let the students eat their snacks during the silent reading time. I rearranged my schedule to accommodate this need.

The snack time was going well. Students brought fruit, veggies, chips, and other types of snacks. One day during snack time, I told the students they could take out their snacks. A student at his desk next to mine took out his snack. He pulled a brown bag from his book bag. He removed his napkin and aluminum foil-wrapped food. He unwrapped the foil to reveal two fried chicken legs and two slices of bread inside. He reached back into his book bag and pulled out a bottle of Louisiana Hot Sauce. He twisted the cap off and splashed several drops of sauce on his chicken legs. All the students stopped what they were doing to watch him prepare his meal. He was content as he arranged his food. After his first bite, he grinned with delight. Some of his classmates giggled at him, but he paid them no mind. He enjoyed his meal happily.

"Yummy, Yummy, Yummy!"

CHAPTER 10

Fallen Bird

Two students came running into my room during recess, screaming, "You have to help us." I told the students to slow down and tell me what was going on. Almost in unison, they said to me that a bird had fallen out of the tree and needed help. "Please help the bird," cried out Jasmine.

We went downstairs, out of the north door, and across the street to the playground. A hurt sparrow was lying on the ground. Many students were huddled around the little bird. I picked up the sparrow and brought it to the classroom. I told one of the students to get me the small box I had on the counter. I placed some tissues in it to give a cushion for the bird to lie. I told Jasmine to go to the 6th-grade science teacher and ask for an eyedropper. I sent Tiffany to the water fountain with a paper cup to fill.

They both returned. I filled the eyedropper with water. I held the bird and tried to give it water with the dropper. The bird did take a couple of drops. I placed the bird back in the box.

Students returned from recess. Jasmine and Tiffany told the students they found a bird on the playground. Many students came to the teacher's desk to view the bird. The bird was still but was breathing.

I told the class to keep their voices down so we wouldn't scare the bird. The students whispered in the classroom. The class atmosphere was of concern for the bird. It was touching.

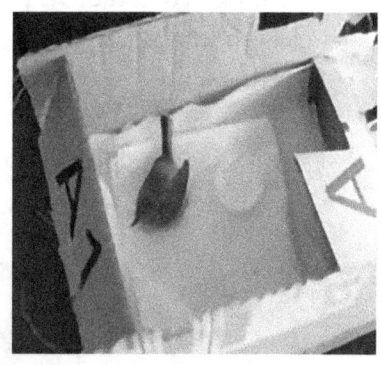

I took the class to lunch, went to the Xerox machine to make copies of a lesson for the students, and chatted with the principal about our morning event with the little bird. Time passed quickly, and it was time to pick the students up from their lunch break.

Unfortunately, upon returning to class, a student noticed that the bird was not breathing. I went over to double-check, and it was true. The little guy was stiff. The room was quiet. One student asked if we could give the bird a funeral. The class chimed in in agreement.

I prepared the bird for burial. I sent a student to find the janitor and ask if he had a shovel. He came upstairs to ask why I needed a shovel. I explained that we had a bird to bury. He volunteered to go outside with us to dig the hole. I told him we were going out after the afternoon recess; it would be just our class outside.

After the afternoon recess, the other classes returned to the building. When the halls were quiet my class went outside. I wrapped the bird in tissue for burial. When we got outside the janitor was already there with a hole in the ground under a tree slightly off school property. He explained that he thought it safer in this area.

I placed the bird in the hole. The janitor covered it up with dirt. One student put a rock at the head of the grave. Only our class would know the significance of this area. We had a little funeral for the sparrow. A few students had thoughtful words to say. We prayed over the bird. A few kids teared up. We stood for a couple of minutes of silence and then retreated to our classroom.

Once we settled in the room, a student raised her hand and said that her grandmother had died. She stated that she went to her funeral. Another student announced that their aunt had passed away a few weeks ago. Listening to the students I thought I'd disregard the last lesson of the day to let the students talk.

I felt grateful that the two girls trusted me enough to help rescue the sparrow.

CHAPTER 11

Right vs Wrong

"Hello, Hello!" I greeted my students. They entered, took their seats, listened to the morning announcements, and stood to recite the pledge over the intercom. Afterward, they sat down and began their morning work while I handled the housekeeping responsibilities.

I taught the language arts lesson, and the students worked silently to complete the assignment. Everyone was quiet and focused. While sitting at my desk reviewing the next lesson, I noticed Michael get up and walk over to John's desk. Michael picked up the army figure that had been standing on John's desk while he was working. He wasn't playing with it; it had simply been there while he worked. Michael made a beeline for John's desk, broke the figure's head off, set it back on the desk, and returned to his seat. John yelled at Michael. I instructed John to come to my desk, and he did. When I questioned him, he had no legitimate response. He replied, "Because I wanted to." I told him he needed to buy another army figure or bring money to pay for the broken toy, apologize to John, and then go sit down. He left my desk, passed by Michael, and yelled, "SORRRRY!" I walked over to John's desk to check on him. I apologized for what happened to his toy and assured him I would make sure he got another one. He dried his tears and said, "Ok."

As the students prepared to go home, I walked up to Michael and reminded him that he needed to buy another army man toy or bring the money. He looked at me and shook his head in understanding. I dismissed the class.

The next day, I arrived early at school. I chatted with Mrs. Franks for a few minutes. I proceeded to my classroom to start my day. I turned on the music and listened as I prepared paperwork for the students.

A large figure lingered at my room door. The man finally bellowed, "Are you, Williams?" I responded. "Can, I help you?" The enormous man and his small wife enter the classroom. I have a round table with chairs for student use. I told them to come in and have a seat. He refused and yelled, "You told my son he must pay for a toy. I'm not paying for a toy."

Mrs. Franks came to the door and asked, "Is everything okay?" I nodded. She went back to her classroom, keeping the door open to listen.

I told the parents that Michael went to John's desk, picked up the toy, and broke the head off. I continued by saying all the students were quietly working at their desks, and Michael chose to be destructive. He continued to yell and curse about what he was not going to do. I let him say what he wanted to say. Then I firmly said, "We are not getting anywhere. If you don't want to calm down, we'll have this conversation in the principal's office." I walked out of my classroom and headed to the principal's office. The parents followed.

I knocked on the door to the principal's office and said I have a situation with a parent. The parents reached Mr. Walker's door, and he told  them to come in. I shared with Mr. Walker the circumstances. Mr. Walker listened.

The father said that he wasn't going to pay. "I don't care if the toy is broken. He shouldn't have had it on his desk. We're not paying for it."

Mr. Walker looked at the parents and asked the father to calm down. Let's come up with a solution. Mom chimed, "Michael said he didn't break the toy." I responded, " All the students were working quietly at their desks. Michael got up from his seat and went directly to John's desk, picked up the army figure, and tore off the head. No one told him to do this. He made and chose this decision and acted on it.

"It wasn't his right to touch another child's property, and he should pay for it." I insisted. Mr. Walker focused on me and said, "Why did he have the toy at school?" I replied, "At the end of the day, students can share things. He brought it to share because his dad is in the military and wanted to talk about it." Mr. Walker retorted, "He shouldn't have had the toy on his desk. Mr. and Mrs. Turner you do not have to pay for it because he shouldn't have had it out. However, Michael cannot touch or destroy other students' property. Can we all agree with that? "No!" I returned. Mr. Turner countered, "That's fine."

Mr. Walker reached his hand out towards Mr. Turner. They shook hands. The parents left the office and the school. Mr. Walker turned, looked at me, and said. " I always like parents to leave my office happy." Fuming, I shared my opinion of disagreeing with his decision. I believe that Michael won't learn from his actions without consequences. But I'll handle it.

I went upstairs to my classroom. Mrs. Franks graciously brought my class in when the bell rang. The students were quietly working on their morning assignments. I thanked her and went inside, closing the door behind me. I called Michael to my desk and instructed him not to get up for any reason unless I called for him, then returned to his desk. The school day passed quickly and there were no incidents.

After school, I went to the toy store and bought an army figure for John. The next day, the students came in. I called John at my desk and presented him with the army figure. He smiled.

I told John, "I know Michael broke your army figure and wasn't going to replace it. It's wrong. So, since you didn't deserve that action, I'm replacing it." John looked at me and smiled. He turned and started back towards his desk. He stopped, turned around, and walked toward me. John looked up at me, said thank you, and gave a great big bear hug.

It was a frustrating situation.

CHAPTER 12

"I've been in Prison."

"Mrs. Williams, you have a phone call," says the secretary over the classroom intercom during my planning time. I go to the office, and she tells me I have Mr. Smith on the phone for you. The secretary mentions that he's upset and has cursed me out. He's in a very hateful mood. I just wanted to give you a heads up. I told her, thanks for the warning.

I went into another small office to take the call. I picked up the phone to say hello and my name. The dad loudly, meanly bellowed, "I just got out of prison and don't have any money to buy my son any glasses. My son doesn't need any fu*king glasses and you stop telling him he does."

The father continued to rant for a few minutes while I listened. When he finished (or got tired of talking), I calmly said, "David can't see and read words on the chalkboard. When reading a book, he has it close to his face to read." Again, Dad asserted that his son doesn't need glasses. I addressed him, "Mr. Smith, your son is a good and hardworking student who is struggling to see. What if I could find a way to get him glasses? I want David to continue to be successful, and the glasses will improve his opportunity. What do you think?" Dad was quiet. There was silence for a few seconds. Dad spoke in a calm and apologetic voice. "I've never heard a teacher say David is a good student. He shared that his son never liked school but is enjoying this year for the first time. Dad told me his wife says she sees improvement in their son's attitude about school. He gets up on time to go to school. He does his homework. The father apologized for his behavior at the beginning of the conversation. By listening to me, he understands that I care about his child's education. He went on to say that the family has been going through financial difficulties for a while. I told him that I understood and would make arrangements for David to get a vision examination and a voucher for his glasses.

At the end of the call, the dad apologized again and said, "Thank you for caring, and God bless you!"

It was a good day.

CHAPTER 13

Great Lakes Star Base

Department of Defense (DOD) Youth Program

The fifth-grade classes went to StarBase in the spring. The experiences of going to the Navy Base for the program were invaluable. We spent one day a week for six weeks. We traveled on a school bus that took us about 4 to 5 miles to the unique adventure.

We spent the school days learning science fundamentals and exploration. The engineering design process gave the students opportunities to think critically and creatively.

Motion and force, and applied technology intrigued the students in the many projects as the students worked cooperatively. They looked forward to StarBase day. All students were in attendance on these days. They came back sharing everything.

Throughout the weeks, the students took part in space simulations, the egg drop challenge, and construction activities. They learned about STEM in multiple fun activities.

There was a couple opportunities to walk the base and see different military areas. The students were always fascinated to see the navy men and women doing drills.

The finale of the program consisted of students launching the rockets they built in teams. This was the cherry on the cake for the students to compete and see which team's rocket goes the highest. All the teams constructed impressive rockets.

This the program offered educational opportunities through multiple hands-on instructional activities. Unfortunately, the teachers learned that the StarBase of Illinois Great Lakes Base was not funded for the future, and the program would be terminated. This was the final year, which we discovered on the last day of class. Students entering fifth grade looked forward to StarBase; it was one of the highlights of fifth grade.

The program was so valuable; it should not have been cut in our state. Bummer!

CHAPTER 14

The Bozo Show

The Bozo Show is housed in the WGN Studio in Chicago and aired for an hour in the mornings five days a week. I entered my class in a school contest to attend the show. We were one of ten schools in Illinois chosen.

I was excited and shared with the class that we were one of ten winners to go to the show. I didn't tell my students earlier because I didn't want to get their hopes up only to not win. The students were thrilled by the news. I informed them of the date and mentioned that I would prepare a field trip slip for them to take home for signatures, and I would also like two parent chaperones to join us.

I prepared the permission slip and contacted the bus company for transportation. As I got ready for the end of the school day, I handed out the permission slips and homework. I informed the students that if their parents wanted to serve as chaperones, they should let me know, and I would reach out to them. I dismissed the class.

The next day, students returned their permission slips. I collected them and noticed that three parents expressed interest in joining us for the show. Throughout the day, I reached out to the parents to thank them for their willingness to accompany us on the field trip.

On field trip day, the students arrived on time and were dressed neatly. Before we boarded the bus, I reminded them of my behavior expectations for both the bus and the show. The parents nodded in agreement. We went downstairs, out the door, and onto the bus. The students greeted the lady bus driver and chose seats in the middle and back. The parents and I also boarded. I spoke with the bus driver and asked if she knew the way to the studio. She confirmed that she did, then started the bus, and off we went.

Our arrival time at the studio was 8:45 am. We left school early to reach the studio on time, allowing for a little wiggle room if necessary. We traveled down Highway 41, then the Edens Expressway, and finally the Kennedy Expressway. We were making good time. The driver exited at the correct exit but made the wrong turn, heading west onto the street. I approached her and pointed out that she had turned the wrong way. She replied that she knew where she was going and had directions. I told her I had directions too and that we should have turned right. She ignored me and insisted, "I will get you there." As we continued westbound, the clock was ticking. After about 5 miles down the road, the driver sheepishly said, "I think I should turn around." Hearing her make that statement, I thought to myself, "No shit Sherlock." But I remained calm and replied, "Okay!" She turned the bus around, and we headed eastbound. Our arrival time was dwindling. We had fifteen minutes to get there, depart the bus, and get into the building before the show started. It wasn't looking good trying to navigate through Chicago's main streets.

We finally pulled up in front of the WGN Studio twenty minutes after the show started. A representative was waiting for us at the front door. Eager to see us, he hurried us off the bus and asked us to be quiet as we entered the studio. We climbed the bleachers and sat without distracting the show.

When the break happened Bozo and Ringmaster Ned came to us and said they were glad we made it. They explained how they could only shoot half of the audience because the other half (us) hadn't made it. Now the camera crew could shoot the entire audience area since it was occupied.

We experienced the Grand Prize Game, which was the bucket game. Every time a ping pong ball goes into six buckets each one farther from the other. The farther the bucket the larger the prize if the ball lands in the bucket. A monetary prize would also be in the last bucket.

We watched comedy skits and cartoons, then chatted after the show. Our class stayed behind once the audience left. Bozo and the crew let us ask questions and get autographs. The class thanks Bozo and the crew. I again told the producer and Ringmaster Ned that I was sorry for our lateness. We shook hands. Afterward, my class, chaperones, and I left the building and boarded the school bus.

As we traveled along the expressways and highways back to school, the students chattered excitedly about their experiences. The chaperones expressed their enjoyment of the trip and their disbelief at being on television. We returned to school just in time for afternoon recess. My students went outside with their peers and shared their Bozo Show adventures.

Before leaving the school, I called the bus company, spoke with the manager, and discussed the bus driver's actions. The manager assured me it would be addressed.

It was a great day!

CHAPTER 15

Robots

Science was enjoyable for my students and me. I brought science to life by integrating hands-on projects into the lessons. Their curiosity and willingness to question things were impressive. If they asked a question I didn't know the answer to, we would find it together.

We had a couple of weeks left before the end of school. We completed the chapters, so I gave the students the option of what kind of science project they would like to do. I gave them a few minutes to ponder this question. I told them we would write the suggestions on the board and vote. After five minutes, I asked for suggestions. Hands raised. Ideas flowed from the students. Once the submissions were written on the board, the students voted. ROBOTS was the winner. I told the class I would give them the criteria for the project tomorrow.

I went home and brainstormed the criteria for the robot project. I created six areas to grade the students.

ROBOTS
Criteria/Rubric

1. Build a robot that can complete a purpose.
2. Robot made from household items, recycle, and electronic.
3. Name of the robot.
4. One page document: explanation of robot choice and decision making, purpose, task(s), and materials.
5. Correct spelling
6. Presentation: Speak clear, eye contact, shows knowledge and confidence

Greeting the students at the door, they came in and sat in their desks. A student rose her hands and asked if I had the robot information for them. I responded, passed out the written directions, and started telling them the criteria. I answered questions. The students were all giddy and excited. I told them the assignment was due in four days. I had them review the criteria and start brainstorming on their robots.

As the days went on, students would ask questions about project. Some students needed encouragement that they were on the right track of their thinking. I told the students I was excited about their robot designs.

ROBOT PRESENTATION DAY....... I looked out the window down at the students as they lined up to come in. The robots varied from small to almost as tall as the students. Everyone had their robots. I went downstairs to retrieve my students first. I gave them a great big smile and told them I was proud to see everyone was prepared. I congratulate all of you!

We came in the room. The students placed their robots on their desk or they were standing next to their desks. After housekeeping and saying the Pledge of Allegiance, we started the presentations. Mr. Walker came into our classroom to see the robots. He told the students he saw the creative

robots on the playground and wanted to learn more about them. Chatter started in the room as the students were surprised to know the principal was interested in their robots.

Mr. Walker sat on the couch at the back of the room and listened attentively to the students' presentations.

As the students presented their robots, they demonstrated that they could perform various tasks, such as doing homework, mowing the lawn, cleaning the house, and much more.

Many robots had simple names like Molly, Burt the Butler, Gizmo, and Einstein.

The students were proud of their robot inventions.

I was happy the students completed the assignment with thought and creativity.

The students presented their robots. I took pictures and completed rubrics for each student. As a finale to their presentations, I called each student up one by one to give them their rubric and participation certificate. All the students clapped for each other. Again, I told them how proud of their creativity in action. Mr. Walker made remarks as well. He came to the front of

the room and stated, "I see future scientists in this class. The future looks bright with you all in it and the contributions you will bring to society. The students had big smiles and puffed out chests with the compliments the PRINCIPAL gave them.

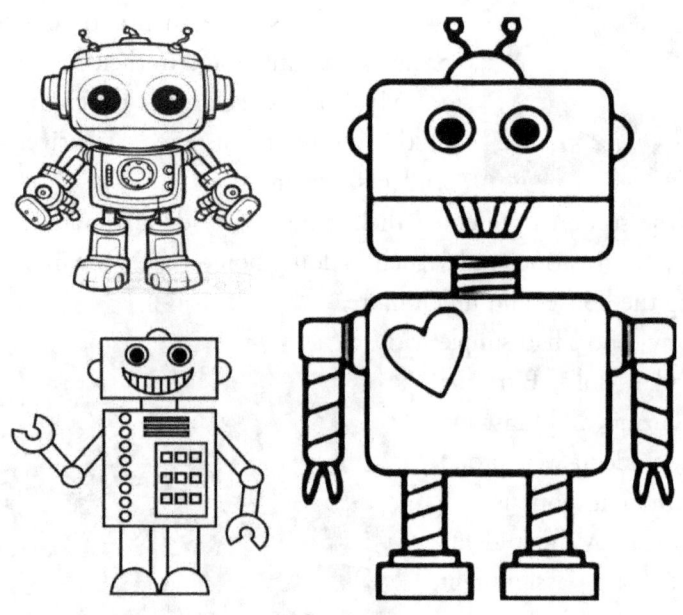

It was a good day!

CHAPTER 16

Passing Grade

This year, I taught fourth grade. Starting a new year is always exciting, and the class worked well together. Throughout the school year, students worked hard, completed assignments, and grew in knowledge.

But I had one student who came to school every day and would never complete his assignments, if he started them at all. He went out of the classroom for special needs support. I even modified his work.

I had taken him aside many times to remind him why he comes to school and the expectations for completing his work. I asked him what he wanted to be when he grew up, and he stated he wanted to be a chef because he loved to cook. I told him the skills he's learning in class would help him become a better chef. We chatted about the responsibilities of being a chef, and he was very knowledgeable. Although the discussion was good, his work habits didn't change.

I chatted with the parents, and they supported the student and his actions. I had never seen anything like it. They were never rude, but they were not stern in insisting that their child improve his behavior. He could read. His math skills were average, I would say. But he wouldn't turn in any work for me to grade.

I sent progress reports home, held conferences, and shared report cards with the parents. All six subjects received "Fs."

I expressed my concerns to the special education director regarding the lack of effort from this student. I told her he hadn't been completing any assignments. I conveyed that I didn't feel comfortable promoting him to the next grade. She responded that I had to pass him. I insisted I couldn't do it; he hadn't earned it. I mentioned that he might be retained in fourth grade. She disagreed, saying, "no, you will not do that." The conversation ended there.

Time passed, and he kept doing the bare minimum or less.

Two weeks before the end of school, I reviewed grades and held mini conferences with each student to discuss their performance. I also allowed students class time to catch up on or complete any assignments that could improve their grades.

The special education director came unannounced to my classroom after school. She wanted to review my grade book, and I gladly gave it to her. She looked at each subject of the unproductive student, then took off her glasses and asked me what grade I was planning on giving him. I'll be giving him all "F"s except for Physical Education; he will be getting a "D" in that class. According to district policy, he hadn't warranted promotion to the next grade.

She told me it would be beneficial for me to pass him. We disagreed for about half an hour. Her attitude changed; her voice became more forceful, and she reminded me that I was not tenured yet.

Well, now she's threatening me without physically doing it. But mentioning tenure threw me for a loop. Why would she bring up tenure? OOOHHHH! Now I get it: do as I say, not what is right. Hummm! I was quiet for a few minutes trying to figure out what to do. I didn't want to lose my position because I didn't do as she directed. After conversing in my head with myself, I said, "ok."

When I recorded student grades three days before the end of the year, I reviewed his report card. I modified his grades to D-'s and promoted him to the next grade level with a notation: "This student is promoted per directive of the Special Education Director."

On the final school day, all the students received their report cards. I wish everyone a wonderful and safe summer. All students were dismissed 30 minutes later.

Glad this year has come to an end!

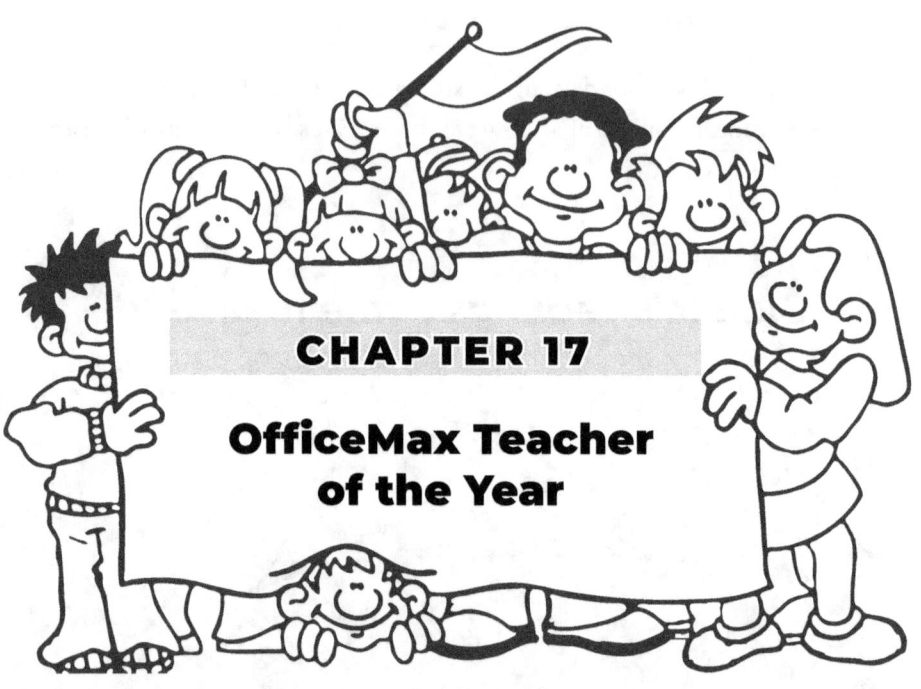

CHAPTER 17

OfficeMax Teacher of the Year

Mr. Comella, the principal, called the classes to the gym for a surprise assembly to recognize students on the honor roll and those with perfect attendance. The third through the sixth grades entered the gym. I brought my class in and directed them where to sit. I had a couple of students sit next to me to keep an eye on them and for them not to distract the other students. The students sat on the floor in a straight row with the teacher sitting in a chair in the same row with an aisle in between. The students chattered while all the classes were getting settled.

The principal comes up to the microphone in front of the audience. He spoke and told the students that this assembly was to honor the students who made the honor roll and perfect attendance. He started with perfect attendance. He called third graders names, then fourth, fifth, and concluded with sixth graders. Each grade level honoree stood as a group for a picture.

The honor roll recipients were called up again according to their grade levels. Students stood for pictures as well. All students returned to their area, and students showed their neighbors their awards.

The principal goes to the microphone and says, " We have one more award to give. We would like to recognize one of our teachers. Office Max Teacher of the Year Award will be recognized this afternoon. As the principal was talking, the back door of the gym opened. A few OfficeMax people came in with items.

I was sitting by the gym door and eyed  the items as they passed me. The last item to come in the door was a nice office chair. I thought to myself, whoever gets these items is very lucky. The teachers looked around at each other not having a clue this teacher's award was to take place. And now you can see the question marks on top of teachers' heads wondering who will be awarded.

The OfficeMax Manager took the microphone and told the audience about the beginnings and purpose of the Teacher of the Year. He stated that the principal has nominated one of our teachers for this award in recognition of their dedication to the students and staff. He went on to mention other attributes of this teacher and concluded by announcing the teacher's name.

While the assembly was going on, I told the two sitting by me to stay still. Then one of the students whispered to me, "Mrs. Williams they called your name." I looked at her with the look of What did you say? The audience clapped. The principal took the mic and said, "Mrs. Williams would you please come to the front so we can present this award to you. Shocked and stunned, I got up slowly and walked towards the front. Everyone clapped and some of the teachers gave me a standing ovation as I continued to move forward. I shook hands with the manager, hugged my principal, and thanked him.

Mr. Comella gave me the microphone and said, "Say a few words." I took the microphone and said a few words. For some reason, I thought I was getting an Academy Award. But I came back to earth and ended by saying thank you.

I felt very appreciated and blessed to be recognized.

CHAPTER 18

I Should Kill You!

When you teach for a few years, you will find yourself teaching siblings of past students. I experienced a family that had several children. I had taught three of them. This family was active in their children's education. They attended school functions, conferences, and were even involved in the school's PTA. A couple of years passed, and I can now teach the last child, Jeff. The youngest of the family has embarked on my class this year. All the siblings of this child were smart and studious. But this last child was a little different.

Jeff was a little slow and didn't care about school too much.

My expectations for the students I taught and teach has always been high and beyond the district's expectations. I believe in challenging their minds and experiences. Well, Jeff was not attentive in class and was easily distracted. I would have to redirect him often throughout the day. He was a little slow on learning skills and mischievious. He wasn't like his older sisters and brother. He was cut from a different cloth. So this child had to be taught with a different approach. However all students were expected to complete all assignments assigned, even if modified. I believe that the world is not tolerant of letting you participate in what is expected, but at times, it overlooks your shortcomings and considers what you can achieve.

So, I always wanted my students to try even if they don't always reach the bar at least move towards it.

As one of my assignments was to write a report on a famous person of their choice. This reports criteria consisted of title page, one to two page report, picture page, reference page, and a report cover. The report had to be typed. So as fourth graders, this shocked a lot of students. I showed them examples of a former student reports. I left the reports on the table for students to review on their free time. I gave them a due date for the reports. They had a week to work on it. I set time during the day for the students to research. The completion had to be done at home.

The students had the weekend to complete their reports. I had expected on Tuesday of the next week.

The weekend and Monday passed. Tuesday came and students were excited about their reports. I told them they would present their reports to the class in the afternoon. Chatter and excitement filled the room. We started the day of subjects and had lunch. Upon returning from lunch, we settled in the classroom and prepared to read the reports.

During the reports the classroom door opened and it was the student's mom. I greeted her and told her to have a seat. I explained the students were presenting their reports. She sat and listened attentively. Her son raised his hand and ask could he read his report. "Yes, please do so." He went to the front of the room and read his report. Before he read, he glanced at his mom, and then started reading his report. When he finished everyone clapped as they did for each report reader. I told the class take a break here and go to recess. We had morning and afternoon recess everyday. The class lined up and we went outside. The mom joined by following behind the students. As they passed through the outside doors, the student scattered in all directions.

The mom walked up to me and said, "I should kill you!" I stopped and turned replying, "Excuse you, what did you say?" She repeated it and continued by saying, "this assignement was so hard for my son. It took the entire weekend to help him with this report. His sister, dad, and I had to assist him in this report. I retorted, "Well, you will have to kill me because my assignments will continue for all students. Now of course, I'll modify for students who needed but all students will complete what is assigned." I reminded her children before this child completed the same report and criteria. I continued to say, "I told your son, he only had to do three-fourths of a page for his famous person, and he started most of it in class. From his presentation, I think he did a good job." The mom dropped her eyes and said, "thank you." But then she looked at me and said, "My family and I went through a difficult time to get him to sit down and stay focused to complete this assignment." I smiled and echoed to her, "Welcome to my world." We both smiled and laughed together.

It was a good day!

CHAPTER 19

Lunch Disruption

I worked with a great group of three fantastic men for about three years. Now, mind you, the eye candy didn't hurt either. I had a new grade-level partner, Fernando, who moved here from California with his family. Our technology teacher, Robert, had been in the district for a while and transferred to our building to teach technology. Derrick was responsible for district technology support and troubleshooting computers as he went around.

Well, Fernando and I went to the computer lab during lunch to talk with Robert about a lesson we wanted to do with our students and needed his help. He was eating his lunch, and we apologized for interrupting him, but we wanted to speak with him. He said he would eat his sandwich while talking with us if we didn't mind. As he ate, we explained that we would assign the students a report and that they needed to conduct research on the computer and then type it up. He agreed to give the students time to work on the assignment.

He invited us to join him for lunch, and we accepted. The next day, Fernando and I brought our lunches to his room, sat at a cleared table, and ate. We talked and laughed. It was a great lunchtime!

The next day in Robert's room, Derrick stopped by to check on the computers. He knocked on the door, and Robert opened it. Derrick stepped inside and remarked that he thought a party was happening. Fernando laughed and said, "No party, but a good time. You should join us." Derrick inspected the computers and took care of what he needed to do. As he walked out the door, he responded, "I just might take you up on the offer. See ya'll later."

The next lunch day, Derrick was already in the room with his lunch. We all chatted about everything under the sun and laughed. Lunch was always a highlight of my day, a time to decompress and relax. The atmosphere was consistently welcoming.

Days, weeks, and months passed during our three years of camaraderie. The support system was excellent. There was no gossip, backstabbing, or negativity—just a great time with people who cared about our students and wanted them to reach their fullest potential.

The fourth year of our lunch pact arrived, but this year was different. Robert's wife transferred to our school, where she taught kindergarten. The kindergarten room was just 25 steps, at most, from the computer room. She could look out her door and see everything that happened, including anyone who entered the computer room.

Lunchtime arrived, and we proceeded to the computer room as usual. Curious eyes observed us as we entered. The first three days went smoothly, but on the fourth day, the door swung open, and in walked the wife with her lunch. The conversations carried on, but the relaxed atmosphere gradually dissipated. During the next lunchtime, the same situation occurred. Robert seemed more withdrawn. Once again, the atmosphere had significantly shifted. I noticed a change in Robert's demeanor; he no longer appeared relaxed. Instead, he looked guarded and cautious.

As the saying goes, he couldn't let loose and be completely himself.

Robert and his wife drove to and from work together daily for years. This year, the pattern remained the same, but the difference was that when she got out of the car, they both walked into the same school at the same time.

Robert had no time to separate, no time alone, and no more joking or laughing. Our lunchtime as a quartet had ended.

Fernando and I took turns visiting each other's rooms to eat together, while Derrick joined us upstairs. We missed Robert's company but understood that it needed to change without explicitly stating it.

Good and memorable times!

CHAPTER 20

Union President

I had been teaching for about five or six years when the music teacher approached me. He asked if I would be interested in becoming a building representative for our district union. He shared that he had been involved for a few years and truly enjoyed it. He mentioned that it's another way to network and meet other people in the state, and he encouraged me to attend a union meeting to observe how it operates.

I had been paying union dues since my first year of teaching. Curious about what was happening with my dues, I thought this might answer my questions. The only time I encountered the union was when we had to vote for representatives, and I once heard about negotiation, voting, and ratifying the contract.

So, I attended the union board meeting with the music teacher. Once there, I saw the PE teacher; she was one of our building reps, like the music teacher. I sat on the side and watched the meeting in action. I saw that there were many people in this setting from different school buildings. I listened to the business as it took place. As the building reps spoke, it seemed like every building had many grievances.

The union president approached me and introduced himself. He asked me if I would think about being a building rep. They tried to get more people active in the organization. I told him I would think about it. I shared that I would come to another meeting to see if I would be interested in this. He replied, "Thanks for coming, and I'll see you next month. And by the way, come to a school board meeting also. We attend those on the third Monday night of each month."

I attended a school board meeting that month. Humm! Interesting.

I attended the union meeting the following month. After sitting there, I thought this couldn't be too hard. I told the president at the end of the meeting that I was interested in becoming a building rep. He replied, "Great! I'll put you on the ballot for next year. Elections took place in May. I was on the ballot. The day after the elections, the results were sent out and shared by the building reps in an after-school union building meeting. I had won the elections with the PE teacher.

I held the building rep status for five years. No one was eager for this position. I represented many grievances over the slightest issues initiated by the teachers and/or principals. The grievances seemed to me like both sides could have sat down and resolved. But, no, it had to be grieved. I fulfilled my responsibility of representing the members.

Again, the union members were paying dues, and we still weren't getting much for our dues. There was always a general meeting at the beginning and a retirement recognition party at the end of the year.

In fairness, I did participate in state conferences, workshops, and even the national convention a couple of times. I learned a lot of information, strategies, and better communication skills. These experiences started nudging me to run for president of our association.

I threw my hat into the race for union president. I made the ballot and won the presidency. The results were four times higher than those of the current president. I guess the association wants or needs a change. This was a position that no one was fighting for. Once I learned the results, I started thinking about how I could differ from the current president's actions. I wanted to bring a new perspective to the organization. I aimed to bring integrity, trustworthiness, renewed confidentiality and ethics, and most importantly, treat everyone equally, regardless of their positions, while acknowledging that we are adults. I truly wanted to shift the old mindset of THEM vs. US. I had heard that phrase too often. I struggled to grasp it because I thought we would all be on the same side, working for the betterment of the students. But it wasn't; it was about the adults. I was determined to change the narrative and mindset.

In late May, I visited the superintendent's office and ran into the district's school board president. He greeted me and offered his congratulations. I responded with a thank you and added, "It's a new day!" I smiled and left.

My challenge begins—the challenge of change is to improve the union. No more THEM vs. US. Let us all work together for the betterment of our clientele, the students. My goals are to increase member involvement, open meeting invitations to all members, strengthen relationships with the district office and the school board, and invite more classified staff to join the union. With our dues, give the members activities, we can all come together and participate. And most of all, decrease the number of grievances around the district.

Let me start by acknowledging that the union executive board and the building representative have been very supportive. The district office and principals slowly but surely began to work more with me to decrease problems that would have led to grievances. We sat down together, talked, and resolved many issues and situations.

All association activities extended invitations to the principals and district office personnel. The executive board put together a back-to-school picnic, character bowling bashes, craft fairs, Association Spelling Bee for 3rd—8th Grades, Association 3rd—8th Grades Honor Roll Awards, Quarterly after-school gathering, and annual retirement party. I met with the superintendent monthly. Negotiations were civil and productive.

I encouraged the secretaries to join the union's ranks. We held a few meetings to provide information about how the union could benefit them.

After addressing their questions and allowing them time to consider it, they voted, and we welcomed them into the association.

We encountered various issues of all kinds, ranging from trivial matters to serious criminal concerns. During my time as president, we addressed only 12 grievances. The past divide of THEM vs US shifted to WE. As a united group from all sides, we accomplished a great deal for our membership, the district, and most importantly, our clientele—the students.

I served as the union president for four two-year terms.

I truly enjoyed the opportunity to serve the membership and district.

CHAPTER 21

BOOM!!!

This new year, I returned excited and pregnant. My pregnancy was progressing well; I was three months along. I taught my students through hands-on activities, presenting skills in creative ways. The students were also attentive and excited.

Months went by, and I was getting bigger; we found ourselves in the middle of the second quarter. I was teaching a math lesson. After the lesson, I began walking around to see if the students needed help and were staying on task. After walking around the classroom for fifteen minutes, I grew tired and returned to my desk. As I slid between the desk and my rolling chair, I attempted to sit down. The chair, however, had other ideas and rolled closer to the window, causing me to land on the floor. SHOCKED AND EMBARRASSED, I sat quietly on the floor. Some students witnessed the incident, but the entire class heard the **BOOM!**

TOTAL SILENCE IN THE CLASSROOM!

As I gathered myself and realized I was not hurt, I laughed. I just had the giggles. Once the students heard me laughing, the silence was broken, and they began laughing too. The ice was broken, and some students rushed to my side to ask if I was okay. I responded, "Yes." As I continued to laugh, the students helped me up, and I pulled the chair close and held onto the seat as I sat down. The students settled down and continued to work on their math assignments. The school day ended, and the students collected their things. I dismissed the class. A few students surrounded me to make sure that I was alright. I assured them I was fine. A couple of them hugged me and told me goodbye.

It was an embarrassing day! LOL

CHAPTER 22

Zzzz ...

Going to school and feeling tired is a common experience for many teachers. For a wife, mom, and teacher who drives an hour to school, the exhaustion can be overwhelming. However, this day was more than just tiring, yet I was still present in my classroom.

I started the class day with one eye open. I handled all the housekeeping duties and provided the students with their morning work to help them get started. While the students were working, I took the first reading group to the back of the room to read.

At the back of the room was a small living area. It featured a compact couch and chairs arranged around it on a rug. The reading group arrived with their books and settled down. I sat on the couch with a student on each side of me. We opened our books to the next story for reading. As part of our routine, the students knew to read three paragraphs, and then the next student on the right would read. This continued until all students had read. Sometimes, I would stop them to discuss what we had read and allow them to share their feedback.

But this morning, sitting on the comfortable couch, sleep called my name. As I held my head down reading along with the students, my eyes began to feel heavy. Despite being tired, the students continued reading. Slowly but surely, my eyes closed. I could hear the students reading, but now my eyes were seeing the insides of my eyelids. It felt like the students were reading extremely slowly, which encouraged me to relax even more.

I heard the door open but paid no attention since a student had asked to go to the washroom. But, as the footsteps seemed different coming in and they did going out. I perked up a little, but not much. Eyes still closed, students kept reading, and the room was quiet.

I heard a student say, "Hi, Mr. Walker! In a semi-slumber state, I heard footsteps moving around the students' desks. Low conversations were taking place with the principal and students. As the footsteps approached the rear, I started to compose myself so I wouldn't be found guilty of sleep.

When Mr. Walker reached the reading area, he said, "Good morning, Mrs. Williams." I lifted my head and responded, "Good morning, Mr. Walker." He questioned the students about the story they were reading, and they answered with many opinions. He stayed for a few more minutes and then departed.

Dodged it, not getting caught semi-sleeping. It was a good day!

CHAPTER 23

"Old Way vs New Way"

Education revolves around various methods of teaching skills. In 2002, No Child Left Behind contributed to the decline of education. In 2010, Common Core negatively impacted education. Every seven to ten years, a new educational initiative is introduced. The 21st Century Skills Initiative is currently in play and may help us get back on track.

When the math concepts changed, I couldn't believe it. Math is a subject that can remain consistent. The goal is to arrive at the right answer and understand how to get there.

Before calculators, math was taught using pencil and paper or figured out in your head. But now there's a new sheriff in town: THE NEW MATH WAY. It takes more time to teach multiple breakdowns in using numbers and symbols to arrive at an answer. The old way of math required anywhere from a minute or less to solve a problem, while the new method takes at least 3 to 6 minutes to find the answer.

I worked hard to understand this absurd new method for solving math problems and teaching it to the students. YUCK!

This is the year to introduce the new math method. It took me four days to teach the students how to multiply two-digit numbers. A few students understood it, so I paired them with those who didn't. This strategy helped me support the students through pairing.

Parent-teacher conferences came around. The most common complaint was the math homework. I told parents we were told to teach this new educational initiative. I shared that the Department of Education had sent out a new Common Core Standards initiative to improve student achievement. Parents' complaints were valid.

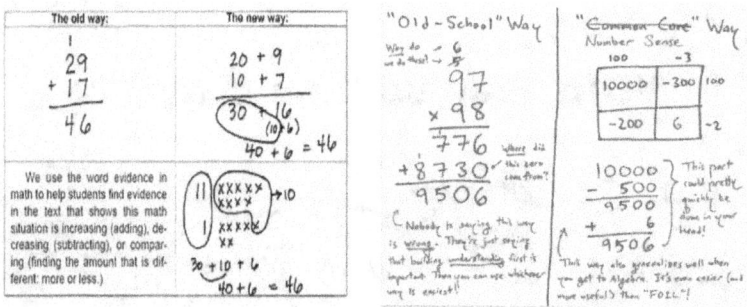

I told several parents that they could teach their child how to solve the math problems as long as the child understood and could explain their reasoning. Go for it! I had no problem if the child provided the correct math answers and showed the process. I assured the parents and students that we would get through this.

Although 21st-century Skills were introduced a few years ago, they have raised a high interest in the global workforce, and students are encouraged to learn and incorporate these skills in all aspects of their subject areas.

Our students still have a chance for a bright future ahead.

CHAPTER 24

Class Pets

After several years of teaching, I decided it was time to introduce a class pet as part of our classroom family. In our first year, we had a pair of hamsters. This allowed the students to take responsibility for the little creatures and provided them with an opportunity to lead a specific classroom task.

The classroom jobs included line leader, attendance/lunch monitor, Pledge of Allegiance monitor, paper passer and collector, hall monitor, bathroom monitor, librarian, emergency drill manager, teacher's assistant, and botanist. Now, we need a zookeeper.

The first classroom pet was two adorable hamsters. When the students came into the classroom, they were excited to see the pair. We took the time to vote on a name for them. I told the students we all take turns caring for the pair. Hands went up to be the first zookeeper. I kept the hamsters for two years and gave it to a student at the end of the year.

Second classroom pet, a salamander. My principal had a pool that had been drained, and he was talking about the salamanders that were in the pool. I asked if I could have one for a class pet. He agreed. I went to his house, and he pulled one out of the pool. I placed it into a small container and took it home. I purchased a habitat for the little guy. It was a nice-sized amphibian.

As a class, they voted on a name.

Since many students had never seen a salamander, they didn't know what it was. I assigned them reports on it for better understanding.

At the end of the year, my class and I walked to a park with a pond. We allowed our pet to roam freely, enjoying the rest of his life.

The third class pet was a white rabbit. Someone had given it to me during the summer. They knew I loved animals and could no longer take care of it, so I gladly accepted it. She provided me with the cage and food.

As cute as the rabbit was, I found myself becoming attached to it. The problem was that I already had a mini zoo at home, which included two dogs, two cats, two cockatiels, two garter snakes, and a boa constrictor. Therefore, I realized the rabbit needed to be a class pet.

On the first day of class, the students were surprised when they walked in to see a white rabbit. After the class settled, I followed the beginning-of-the-year welcoming routine for the students. Afterwards, I introduced the rabbit, who already had a name, Hoppy. That's how he was introduced. The students excitedly expressed their desire to be zookeepers. I assured them that everyone would have a chance.

When the janitor came in, he saw the rabbit and laughed. "He will fit well in my big pot for dinner," said the custodian. The class gasped. I responded, saying, "What? Are you crazy? Don't talk about Hoppy like that." "Hoppy? Hoppy can hop right into my pot. Ha ha ha!" he chuckled.

I asked the custodian, "If I leave Hoppy over the weekend, would you check on him for me?" He said, "You're sure you want me to do that?" "Yes!" "I'll take good care of Hoppy over the weekend for you, Ms. Williams." "I'd appreciate that." The class thanked him for agreeing.

Students brought carrots, lettuce, and other treats for the rabbit. Hoppy was doing well. I thought I might let him out of the cage to stretch his legs. I closed the door, and he roamed freely around the room. After a couple of months in the building, when all the students on the second floor knew him well, I made a big move. I left the door open so he could venture into the hallway. The other students were delighted to see him. Everyone made sure Hoppy was safe. Hoppy never went near the stairs and often returned to the room when he got tired, or a student from another class would escort him back to his homeroom.

As Hoppy familiarized himself with all the classrooms, he seemed to favor one teacher's room. He would always go to her room and find his favorite corner. Then Hoppy started to poop in that corner.

At first, the teacher said she didn't mind because she thought it was an accident, but now he's making it a routine, and could I please keep him in my room? I obliged her. Well, that lasted about four days until the other students said they missed seeing Hoppy. So, I let Hoppy roam free in the halls. The teacher who complained saw Hoppy coming toward her classroom and immediately returned to her room, closing the door.

Hoppy had a wonderful year with the class. The following school year, the students were already familiar with Hoppy, making the transition to becoming zookeepers smooth for them. This year, I expanded the zookeepers' responsibilities and allowed the students to take Hoppy home over the weekends and during holiday breaks. Everything went well until the last home visit. The student, unfortunately, had to walk Hoppy back to school in the cold. Although Hoppy had a nice furry coat, I doubt it kept him warm enough for the walk. A couple of days later, Hoppy passed away in the classroom during class time. One student noticed Hoppy was lying still and not moving. I checked on him, and he was deceased. We all cried. Some students blamed the girl who took him home, but I assured them that it wasn't anyone's fault; it must have been Hoppy's time to go to rabbit heaven.

As much as I loved Hoppy, it hit me hard. I decided against having any more class pets. We held a funeral for Hoppy and buried him next to the bird I had buried years ago. We all said our goodbyes and returned to the classroom.

It was a sad day!

R.I.P. Hoppy

CHAPTER 25

The Decision to Move to Jr. High School

I have taught third, fourth, and fifth grades for twenty-six years. I remember contemplating how to positively impact children's lives. I was determined to teach. In the beginning, I felt both excited and nervous as I walked into the empty classroom with the teaching materials provided by my principal. After many years of teaching, I have cherished watching my students become engaged and learn from my creative style and educational approach. Teaching is my passion.

However, the educational system's focus gradually shifted toward test preparation, testing, and passing tests. There were no longer any science or social studies classes, or additional subject-related projects. As the years went by, testing became the priority. After several years of this, my enthusiasm for teaching began to diminish.

I asked the superintendent if there were any teaching positions available at the middle school. He mentioned they had an opening in the life skills class, which had seen a revolving door of substitutes. Several substitute teachers had come and gone. The course seemed unappealing to teachers and failed to engage seventh- and eighth-grade students.

to be continued...

Please, Read Book 2

www.ingramcontent.com/pod-product-compliance
Lightning Source LLC
Chambersburg PA
CBHW071542120626
46550CB00006B/2541